KITCHEN SINK DRAMA

A Play

A N D R E W B I S S

Original cover images © canstockphoto/snip

Cover design by Ernest Waggenheim

First Printing, 2017

ISBN-13: 978-1546771364
ISBN-10: 1546771360

ENTR'ACTE
EDITIONS

"The dangers of life are infinite, and among them is safety."

~ Goethe

TABLE OF CONTENTS

CHARACTERS

GRAHAM WAVERING: A mild-mannered pragmatist, disciplined and objective with an inherent sense of optimism. Nondescript in appearance. Mid-fifties.

ELAINE WAVERING: Graham's wife. A world-weary malcontent with an acerbic edge that belies a timid core. Rather homespun in appearance but not unattractive. Early-fifties.

JOY: Elaine's sister. A self-possessed, independent thinker. Very attractive, stylish and brutally forthright. A well-kept late-forties.

MAN: Happy-go-lucky, playfully sarcastic and blatantly flirtatious. Good-looking. Early-twenties.

SETTING & TIME

SETTING: The kitchen of the Wavering's suburban London home.

TIME: Act I, Scene 1: Early morning, the present.
            Act I, Scene 2: Later that afternoon.
            Act I, Scene 3: Afternoon, the following day.

            Act II, Scene 1: Midday, two weeks later.
            Act II, Scene 2: Early morning, six months later.
            Act II, Scene 3: Early morning, several months later.

ACT I

Scene 1

At Rise: The kitchen of GRAHAM and ELAINE WAVERING'S home in a quiet London suburb. At rise GRAHAM is seated at the kitchen table consuming the remainder of his breakfast while reading a newspaper. Shortly thereafter, ELAINE appears in the doorway L., looking tired and irritable. She remains there for several moments staring at GRAHAM before entering.

ELAINE: (*Morosely.*) Morning, darling.

GRAHAM: (*In singsong fashion, without looking up.*) Good morning!

ELAINE: (*As she meanders over to the countertop.*) Ughh!

GRAHAM: And how *are* we today?

ELAINE: (*Despondently.*) Us? We're on top of the world.

GRAHAM: (*Reverting back to his newspaper.*) Jolly good – that's what I like to hear.

ELAINE: Christ, Graham, honestly – must you really be so pleasant and agreeable first thing in the morning – you know how grating I find it. (*As she fetches herself a cup and saucer.*) Any tea left?

GRAHAM: (*Brightly.*) I'm sure there's a cup or two more to be squeezed.

    (ELAINE *pours tea for herself, as* GRAHAM *continues with his newspaper.)*

ELAINE: By the way, the waste disposal's broken again.

GRAHAM: *(Breezily.)* Oh. Well, not to worry – I'll call someone when I get to the office.

ELAINE: What have you got to be so chirpy about, anyway? Did you wake up and forget who you were?

GRAHAM: No particular reason, darling; just an overall sense of gratitude for the opportunity of spending another day on this magnificent blue sphere of ours.

ELAINE: God, you make me wish I'd never gotten up. I know you do it just to annoy me. Any sane-minded person would swear you were drunk.

GRAHAM: Horribly drunk, I'm afraid – on life's heady aroma.

ELAINE: Oh, for heaven's sake, stop it! You're becoming unbearable.

GRAHAM: *(Contritely.)* Sorry, dear.

> *(GRAHAM continues to peruse the newspaper as ELAINE sips her tea, eyeing him suspiciously. Pause.)*

ELAINE: Am I to assume, from your nauseating high spirits that for the first time in the history of mankind there is actually a snippet of good news in the paper?

GRAHAM: *(Without looking up.)* No, no – no good news, I'm afraid. Just the usual. *(Scanning the front page.)* Let's see…death, corporate sleaze, political sleaze, more death, another child abducted in Coventry, death again, some ex-pop star about to host a talk show, death, death, death…oh, yes, and the Italian's have elected a new prime minister.

ELAINE: (*Wearily.*) For God's sake, every day the same bloody thing.

GRAHAM: More or less.

ELAINE: It's like treading water in a stagnant pond; the same slop churning up around you. I mean, honestly, what's the point?

GRAHAM: I'm not entirely sure that there is one, is there? Does there have to be one?

ELAINE: Of course there does. I don't want to have gone through all of this for nothing.

GRAHAM: (*After a moment of contemplation.*) Then perhaps the 'going through' is the point.

ELAINE: God, how depressing! Why do you say things like that – apart from wishing to inflict emotional damage upon me, that is?

GRAHAM: Think of it as a journey. Don't worry about what's at the other end, just enjoy the getting there.

ELAINE: What journey? I'm on no journey. I got a flat tire in the middle of nowhere years ago, and I'm still standing by the side of the bloody road with a pathetic look on my face.

GRAHAM: Anything left in the pot?

3

ELAINE: No. It's all used up. We're all used up.

GRAHAM: Not to worry.

ELAINE: (*Testily.*) Well, you should worry.

GRAHAM: I don't see why?

ELAINE: Because you wanted another cup and now you can't have one. You should be marginally pissed off at the very least.

GRAHAM: Oh, I'm sorry; did you want another cup?

ELAINE: No!

GRAHAM: Then why get so upset?

ELAINE: Because you did and you're not!

GRAHAM: Me? Oh, I don't mind, really. It'll probably save me a trip to the loo on the train, I expect.

ELAINE: (*Resentfully.*) God, it's all so easy for you, isn't it?

GRAHAM: What is?

ELAINE: *This!* This whole bloody…whatever this is. You just blithely steer your way through it all, with your sails billowing, and your little cap on, waving at all your fellow travelers without a care in the world. God, you make me sick sometimes, you *really* do.

GRAHAM: Well…I suppose I was a *little* disappointed that there wasn't another cup left in the pot…if that helps?

ELAINE: No, it doesn't! What would help is if you'd stop being so happy and easy-going all the bloody time. Life's hard enough, without that. Why can't you be more cynical? I'd have a damned sight more respect for you if you were.

GRAHAM: Very well, darling, if it'll make you happy, I shall, from here on, endevour to cultivate the more self-destructive elements of my personality.

ELAINE: Rubbish! You don't have any. And besides, that answer in itself gives lie to your intentions; you'd say just about anything to appease or acquiesce. Why your mother didn't name you Neville I shall never know.

(*Pause.*)

GRAHAM: (*Without looking up.*) Did you not sleep well, darling?

ELAINE: What a stupid question – you know I never sleep well. Even the pills have become useless – my system has finally wrestled them to the ground. (*Beat.*) You, on the other hand, doubtless slept like a baby.

(*Pause.*)

GRAHAM: Actually, no, I…I had a rather…fractured nights sleep, as a matter of fact.

ELAINE: (*Mockingly.*): Oh? Fractured? How horrifying! And why was that, pray tell?

GRAHAM: Oh…nothing, really.

ELAINE: Had a nightmare in which you actually found yourself having to take a stand on something?

GRAHAM: No, not a nightmare. Just a dream. Rather a pleasant dream, actually. Very pleasant. And yet…a little disconcerting at the same time.

ELAINE: (*Impressed.*) Disconcerting?

GRAHAM: After the fact, yes.

ELAINE: Well?

GRAHAM: I…I believe I'd rather not discuss it in detail, if it's all the same to you.

ELAINE: It's not all the same to me. Good God, having you say that something is disconcerting and you'd rather not discuss it is like hearing David Attenborough admit to having had sex with animals. Now come on, out with it!

(*Pause.*)

GRAHAM: No, I…I, I truly believe that it's something that's best not put under the microscope…given our circumstances. Suffice to say that my sleep pattern was not on par with its usual timetable last night.

ELAINE: What do you mean, "our circumstances"? We don't have any. We never have – that's the problem. Now, just tell me whatever it is that you dreamt.

GRAHAM: Elaine, please.

ELAINE: (*Firmly.*) Please what?

GRAHAM: (*Ingenuously*.) Please sir?

ELAINE: There's no need to be nasty.

GRAHAM: Elaine, please don't make me.

ELAINE: (*Knowingly*.) Oh. (*Beat*.) Oh, now I understand. You sly bastard. So you give me a little teaser and then I'm supposed to insist and insist until you've finally told me whatever it is that you dreamt, and then whatever it is – however much I might loathe it – will be mitigated by the fact that I kept on insisting to know, despite your pleas to the contrary. Consequently, I become the aggressor and you appear as the oppressed victim, bullied into a confession under my unrelenting duress. My God, you're cunning. You really are a piece of work, do you know that?

GRAHAM: Elaine, I've a feeling that you're reading far more into this than is actually there.

ELAINE: I'm not reading anything into anything; you haven't told me anything – despite my *barbaric* interrogation. I mean, if it's all so hideous why don't you just call Amnesty International right now and tell them all about me?

GRAHAM: Elaine–

ELAINE: Go public, I don't care…I'll tell them *everything* I know.

GRAHAM: Elaine, it was just a dream.

ELAINE: Then, if it was just a dream why won't you tell me about it?

GRAHAM: I'm…I'm not entirely certain that it's the sort of

thing one discusses over breakfast.

ELAINE: Oh, stop being so precious – you've just eaten slices of flesh from a dead carcass and a couple of embryonic birds.

GRAHAM: Nonetheless–

ELAINE: Anyway, you've finished and I'm not having any, so I say let it all hang out.

GRAHAM: Elaine, must you be so vulgar?

ELAINE: Vulgar? What's vulgar about that? There's nothing vulgar in my words, only in your interpretation, and I can hardly be held responsible for that.

GRAHAM: All right, all right, but... (*Beat.*) Before I say anything more, please understand that my reticence is born not from any sense of wrongdoing, but from a place of...naiveté.

ELAINE: Well, that I *can* believe.

GRAHAM: No. I mean it.

ELAINE: I know you do, darling, and I completely understand. I am your wife, after all – who'd know better than me? And by the way, this is becoming more intriguing by the second. I never knew you had a dark side. It almost makes you a little bit...I don't know...sexy.

GRAHAM: Oh, don't say that – now I'm not sure that I should.

ELAINE: For God's sake, of course you should. Now, be a man, make a decision and stand by it.

GRAHAM: All right. (*Beat.*) All right, if you insist on knowing, I had a dream about…about a man. Rather a young man…with a ponytail.

ELAINE: And?

GRAHAM: And we… (*Decisively.*) In this dream, we… we had…certain relations.

ELAINE: (*Rolling her eyes.*) What's so shocking in that? Relations aren't *that* peculiar…well, one or two of mine are, but that's beside the point.

GRAHAM: That's not what I meant.

ELAINE: Then, what?

GRAHAM: Elaine, we had…sexual relations.

(*Pause.*)

ELAINE: I see. (*Beat.*) And I assume by that you're not referring to wanton aunts and uncles?

GRAHAM: No.

ELAINE: No, I…I thought not.

GRAHAM: Good.

(*Pause.*)

ELAINE: I see. (*Beat.*) So…you and this young man…

GRAHAM: Yes.

ELAINE: With a ponytail…

GRAHAM: Yes.

(*Pause.*)

ELAINE: And did you…did you enjoy it?

GRAHAM: (*Taking a deep breath.*) I would have to say…I would have to say that…that, yes, indeed I did.

ELAINE: I see. (*Beat.*) And did he?

GRAHAM: He appeared to.

ELAINE: Meaning what, precisely?

GRAHAM: Meaning that…that his reactions – both physical and vocal – led me to believe that he did, in fact, find the experience to be gratifying in nature.

ELAINE: I see. (*Beat.*) And have you had such dreams before?

GRAHAM: Never.

ELAINE: I see. (*Beat.*) And you say you enjoyed it?

GRAHAM: Yes…to a surprising degree.

ELAINE: Though, perhaps not to quite such a degree of surprise as my own. (*Beat.*) And what do you intend to do about it?

GRAHAM: Do about it?

ELAINE: Yes…do about it.

GRAHAM: Nothing, of course. It was just a dream. It came, it went.

ELAINE: You conquered.

GRAHAM: I knew I shouldn't have told you.

ELAINE: No, you were quite right to do so.

GRAHAM: Look, Elaine, I can't explain it. I've never had a dream like that before; I've never had feelings like that before…never. But last night, for some unknown, bizarre reason, I did. I can't rationalize it, I can't excuse it, and I can't deny it. But last night – in my dreams – I had sexual relations with a young man with a ponytail. Who would ever have thought it? Certainly not me. But I did. And I found it – to my astonishment – to be very pleasurable, and so did he. Now please, let's put this matter to rest and discuss something more suitable.

ELAINE: Put it to rest! How can I? And how dare you suggest that I should.

GRAHAM: Elaine, I think I've been more than fair with you on this. I've admitted that I found it deeply gratifying – that in itself is a considerable concession. I've also admitted that I found myself at something of a crossroads…well, not exactly a crossroads, more of a…bump in the road. And now I've had that bump, and it's over. So please let's just move along.

ELAINE: "Deeply gratifying"? Every time you mention it, it

becomes a little more raunchy. First you enjoyed it, then it was pleasurable, and now it's "deeply gratifying."

GRAHAM: That is because, Elaine, it *was* deeply gratifying...*in my dream.* The first dream that I have ever had in my entire life where I found myself engaged in sexual activity with a person of...a comparable sex. Did I enjoy it? Yes, very much so. Do I hope to have similar dreams in the future? No, not at all. Can I explain this subconscious anomaly? If only I could.

ELAINE: And what exactly was it about it that you enjoyed?

GRAHAM: Elaine, it never happened, so why torture yourself with figments from my imagination?

ELAINE: (*With a nervous laugh.*) Torture myself? Good God, darling, you make me sound like a pregnant teenager, gazing at a Polaroid of some pimply brute who'd promised eternal devotion. I mean, I love you and everything, but it's not as if we're *in* love, for pity's sake. I just want to know the ins and outs of it. I promise I won't faint.

GRAHAM: Ins and outs?

ELAINE: Or ups and downs.

GRAHAM: Elaine, I truly feel that this line of questioning goes beyond the bounds of marital badinage and encroaches upon my personal privacy as an individual. Now, please, just let it lie.

ELAINE: Did he kiss you?

GRAHAM: Elaine!

ELAINE: Did he?

GRAHAM: (*With a sigh.*) Not on the lips.

ELAINE: Where, then?

GRAHAM: Elaine, please.

ELAINE: Where?

GRAHAM: Elaine, *please.*

ELAINE: *Where?*

(*Pause.*)

GRAHAM: In and around my groin area.

(*Beat.*)

ELAINE: I see. (*Beat.*) And did you kiss him?

GRAHAM: No…not on the lips.

ELAINE: Then, where?

GRAHAM: Elaine!

ELAINE: *Where?*

GRAHAM: Elaine, it's not something–

ELAINE: (*Forcefully.*) Where?

(Beat.)

GRAHAM: I kissed him…on the shaft and head of his penis.

(Pause.)

ELAINE: I do believe that that is the first time in my entire life that I have ever heard those words strung together in a sentence. Not that I didn't expect to, necessarily, I just…never imagined hearing them from you. *(Beat.)* And did he enjoy it?

GRAHAM: Why do you keep asking that?

ELAINE: Did he?

GRAHAM: He didn't say so, in so many words.

ELAINE: But?

GRAHAM: But judging from the guttural reactions I recall hearing at the time, I would have to conclude that, yes, in all probability, he did.

ELAINE: And what else did you do?

GRAHAM: Elaine, I believe I've been more than candid already; please don't pursue this any longer.

ELAINE: I have a right to know.

GRAHAM: What right? It was *my* dream.

ELAINE: But I'm your wife.

GRAHAM: But it never really happened.

ELAINE: So why not tell me?

GRAHAM: Because I…

ELAINE: Did you have intercourse?

GRAHAM: *Elaine!*

ELAINE: Did you?

GRAHAM: I refuse to answer. That is utterly beyond the limits of reasonable curiosity.

ELAINE: Did you?

> (*GRAHAM remains silent. ELAINE speaks in a very deliberate tone.*)

ELAINE: I shall ask you one more time, Graham, and I expect you to answer me. If you do not, then I shall be forced to resort to more desperate tactics. (*Firmly.*) Now, did you have intercourse?

> (*Pause.*)

GRAHAM: (*Hesitantly.*) Yes…but only briefly.

> (*Beat.*)

ELAINE: And what was…who…what role did you play?

GRAHAM: I played a…a passive role.

ELAINE: (*With an air of sadness.*) Yes…yes, I can see that, at least.

GRAHAM: But it was very brief.

ELAINE: And did you…did you find that pleasurable, too?

GRAHAM: I…I would have to say that…that if you truly cannot live without knowing every intimate detail of my very private and entirely fictional subconscious brain activity, then…then, yes, I did indeed find the experience pleasurable. (*With great import.*) *In context.*

(*Beat.*)

ELAINE: Oh, by the way, your mother called while you were in the shower.

GRAHAM: My mother?

ELAINE: Yes.

GRAHAM: What did she want?

ELAINE: I've no idea – she didn't say.

GRAHAM: Well, never mind, I'll call her from the office.

(*Pause.*)

ELAINE: What was his name?

GRAHAM: Who?

ELAINE: This boy with the ponytail?

GRAHAM: I've no idea – he didn't say.

ELAINE: How odd?

GRAHAM: How so?

ELAINE: To be so intimate, and yet so…anonymous.

GRAHAM: I don't know that strangers in your dreams ever do have names, do they?

ELAINE: (*Upon reflection.*) I suppose not. (*Beat.*) Still, to have kissed his penis and not even known his name…

GRAHAM: Elaine, really! I insist that you desist. I've admitted to a troubled nights sleep and I've admitted to the cause. It was a private, intimate moment that I revealed to you in what I would describe as more than generous terms. The least you could do is grant me the courtesy of finding a new point of reference for our discourse.

ELAINE: Are we having discourse? After the night you had, I'm surprised you still have the energy. (*Beat.*) What did you talk about, by the way?

GRAHAM: (*Becoming testy.*) What? Oh, I don't know – what does it matter? I don't know that we did talk.

ELAINE: How primal. No wonder it was so deeply gratifying.

GRAHAM: (*Suddenly standing.*) I'm sorry, Elaine, but this atmosphere has become completely intolerable. I'm leaving for work – I shall see you this evening.

ELAINE: Very well, darling – have a wonderful day.

(*GRAHAM crosses to ELAINE and gives her a perfunctory kiss on the cheek.*)

GRAHAM: And honestly, you mustn't worry – there's certain to be some tedious university study somewhere that gives credence to the depressing normality of it all, you mark my words.

ELAINE: Yes, I'm sure there is, darling…at the University of Morocco, I expect.

GRAHAM: (*As he's exiting.*) Just don't forget what I said, that's all.

(*GRAHAM exits through the door L. Momentarily the front door is heard slamming shut. Beat.*)

ELAINE: I sincerely doubt there's any fear of that.

(*The lights fade to BLACK.*)

Scene 2

Later that same day. ELAINE is sitting in a chair at the kitchen table, book in hand, snacking from a bowl of something on the table. Momentarily the sound of a doorbell is heard. ELAINE, in a state of agitation, rushes to answer the door.

ELAINE: (*Off.*) Oh, Joy! Thank God! I've been waiting an eternity. I was starting to think you'd gone all peculiar on me, too. It's been an eon at least since I called.

(*JOY enters, speaking in rapid-fire sentences, followed by ELAINE.*)

JOY: Darling, my apologies, you must forgive me, but it's Wednesday, as you know – the day I have to take Stephen's brats to the park – hideous, I know, but what can you do? And so there I am, sitting on this hideously uncomfortable wooden bench that's covered in lichen and bird shit, being subjected to the most appalling high-pitched squeals and laughter emanating from those pre-pubescent monsters from Stephen's squalid little pre-me marriage, wondering what the hell I'd done to deserve it all, when I attempt – in desperation – to make contact with the outside world and check my messages, and wouldn't you know it…the damned phone's out of juice. So, then I have to drag these two creatures, kicking and screaming needless to say, to the nearest wine bar where I can plug in and recharge – me and the bloody phone – them crying and sobbing the whole three hours, of course – even though I'd bought them more magazines and fizzy drinks than you could possibly imagine – until I finally get a signal, got your hideous message, unloaded the brats back onto Stephen and charged over here as if my life depended on it. So how are you, darling? Well, obviously you're feeling completely hideous – but, I mean, other than that? Is everything all right?

ELAINE: Yes, everything's fine, really…other than that.

JOY: Well, that's a relief at least. Thank God for small mercies, I say. (*Beat.*) So…what's the problem?

ELAINE: It's Graham.

JOY: Oh God, not again. What is it now? Don't tell me…you found another brown stain in his underwear.

ELAINE: No, Joy, it's…it's far more disturbing, I'm afraid.

JOY: Then what colour is it?

ELAINE: It isn't a colour. It has nothing to do with his underwear. Well…not really…I mean, it might do…in some ways…but not really…as far as I can tell.

JOY: Darling, I do apologise, but I've had a very long and very arduous day, so I'm afraid you're going to have to be substantially more specific if this conversation is to hold my attention. Now, does Graham's underwear factor in to your predicament or doesn't it?

(*Beat.*)

ELAINE: No.

JOY: Good, now that's clear, at least. So what does?

(*Beat.*)

ELAINE: His…his lover.

JOY: Oh, God – I knew it!

ELAINE: How did you know?

JOY: I don't know…just one of those things one says, I suppose. (*Beat.*) Are you positive?

ELAINE: Yes, he's told me everything.

JOY: That was very forthright of him. Quite out of character, if you'll forgive my saying so, but there it is.

ELAINE: No, no, completely. Under duress, of course.

JOY: Of course. And what's her name?

ELAINE: It's not a "her."

JOY: What do you mean, "it's not a her."

ELAINE: I mean, it's a "him."

JOY: Well, of course it's a "him." If it's not a "her," then there's not much else it could be, is there?

ELAINE: Then why ask?

JOY: I don't know – just one of those things one says, I suppose.

ELAINE: And?

JOY: And what?

ELAINE: Aren't you appalled?

JOY: No.

ELAINE: Why ever not?

JOY: Should I be?

ELAINE: He's having an affair.

JOY: With a man.

ELAINE: Precisely.

JOY: Precisely.

ELAINE: Joy, I'm your sister – I'm reaching out to you – at least *try* to grab my bloody hand!

JOY: But I am, darling. You just told me he's having an affair with a man.

ELAINE: Exactly.

JOY: So, why worry?

ELAINE: Why worry!

JOY: Yes. In fact, you should be pleased.

ELAINE: Pleased!

JOY: Yes – that it's a man.

(*Beat.*)

ELAINE: (*Bemused.*) I'm…I'm sorry, I don't follow.

JOY: Well, darling, if he's having an affair with another man then there's really nothing to worry about, is there? I mean, I'm assuming, of course, the marriage is sexless?

ELAINE: (*Defensively.*) No more than the norm.

JOY: Well, there you are.

ELAINE: Where?

JOY: Where you should be.

ELAINE: I still don't understand.

JOY: Look, darling, he's only human, after all – hard to imagine sometimes, but there you are. And more to the point, he has needs along with the rest of us – though frankly, that's even harder to imagine.

ELAINE: Joy, how can you be so blasé about it? This is my life…in crisis!

JOY: Oh, for God's sake stop going on like some button-downed hausfrau. Just stop for a second, take a deep breath, and have a good hard look at yourself: You're of a certain age; you and Graham have been married for…God knows how long…

ELAINE: Twenty-three years.

JOY: Twenty-three years; you no longer find each other sexually appealing – and on the odd occasion you feel obliged to do so, it's more than likely forced and horrid; there's doubtless very little left in that burnt out ember of love that, with great force of mind, I can only vaguely imagine you once shared; and what little conversation you continue to exchange is almost certainly argumentative and combative, or else so dull and predictable that both of you have trouble summoning the energy to respond, since you both already assume to know what the other's going to say before the sentence has hardly begun. Am I right?

(*Beat.*)

ELAINE: What if you were?

JOY: So, what do you expect? These things are going to happen.

ELAINE: Well, perhaps they are, but…but I still don't understand how you can be so matter-of-fact about Graham being with another man.

JOY: Darling, he's just scratching an itch. You know men and sex; it's like going to the lavatory – they'll do it just about anywhere when the urge is strong enough.

ELAINE: (*Unconvinced.*) I suppose so.

JOY: Of course so. Look at the prison system, for God's sake – it's a virtual World's Fair of heterosexual buggery.

ELAINE: Even so…it's still not right…it's still cheating.

JOY: Oh, for Christ's sake, listen to you – prattling on like some horn-rimmed hangover from the 1950s. It's a part of life, for heaven's sake – haven't you figured that out yet? I mean, how old are you? (*Beat.*) Anyway, it doesn't count with another man – it's just sex. If he were banging some opportunistic little sex kitten I'd see more cause for concern. I mean, let's face it, you're losing what few looks you once had – I hate to say it, darling, but there it is – your personality's a non-starter, and you've absolutely no trade skills. Your entire future would hinge upon some greasy little solicitor. But, luckily for you, Graham isn't banging some little kitten; he's merely…exercising his options.

ELAINE: I don't care what you say, it's still not right. And besides, why should he be the one to have all the excitement? It's me whose life is in a rut. I'm the one stuck in this miserable bloody house all day, summoning ways to fill this void that I laughingly call "my life." I'm the one starving for a little diversion, for God's sake.

JOY: So, what exactly is it that bothers you– the gender preference or the humping in general?

ELAINE: Both. (*Pause.*) The humping.

JOY: (*Impatiently.*) Then you've only yourself to blame.

ELAINE: What a ridiculous, and, may I say, very hurtful thing to say.

JOY: Elaine, life does not come to you – you must go to it. If you want more excitement in your life, then I'm afraid you're going to have to make a little bit more of an effort – unless, of course, you're content to mope around here like some Chekhovian drudge for the rest of your life.

ELAINE: What are you suggesting?

JOY: Nothing. I'm merely pointing out that Graham – in all his Grahamness – has somehow managed to inject a little colour into his drab life whilst still maintaining the status quo. If you lack the initiative to do the same then that's your business, but for Christ's sake stop pointing your finger at other people like some miserable martyred blob of inertia.

ELAINE: You're saying I should cheat on him?

JOY: I refer back to my last statement.

ELAINE: So, you are?

JOY: (*Her patience nearing an end.*) Oh, for God's sake, Elaine – "cheat"? What the hell does that mean? What sort of Sesame Street mentality do you live by? It's just a word. A word that describes not living by the rules, and if you choose to live the rest of your life living by the rules, then…then, best of luck, darling.

ELAINE: (*Stridently.*) I have always tried to live my life in a–

JOY: You live your life in an emotionless, sexless marriage. You don't have a loving relationship, you have a husband and a house – both of which are semi-detached – and if you're so hamstrung by your own misguided Girl Scout morality that you can't see the wood for the trees, then…then stop leaving hysterical messages on my cell phone.

ELAINE: (*Reprovingly.*) I wonder what Stephen would say if he could hear you now.

JOY: Probably exactly what I'm saying.

ELAINE: I doubt that very much.

JOY: Do you? Well, in that case, why don't you ask one of his tarts…or better yet, ask one of mine.

(*Beat.*)

ELAINE: You mean, you…both of you…

JOY: Get it? Yes. We don't involve each other in it. To all intents and purposes we live a perfectly normal married life. But we've both found ways to…fill in the blanks without spoiling the puzzle.

ELAINE: Exactly – you cheat at the puzzle.

JOY: We both take a peek in the dictionary once in a while, when the other's not looking. It's not cheating, it's…keeping the game in play. Look, it's not that complicated. In fact, it's not complicated at all. I can't imagine living my life without Stephen in it, nor he me, presumably. We wish to remain together. Therefore, we acknowledge and accept those occasional liberties that will enable us to continue doing so. Make sense?

ELAINE: But you…you seemed so content, you and Stephen?

JOY: *We are*, that's just it!

ELAINE: But, doesn't he…

JOY: No.

ELAINE: Aren't you…

JOY: No.

ELAINE: But he has to…

JOY: No, he doesn't – and neither do I.

(*Beat.*)

ELAINE: But it can't be as easy as all that. Life's not that simple.

JOY: Life is very simple, darling: you live, you breathe, you die – that's it. Whatever you choose to do with the rest of it is entirely up to you. It's only as complicated as you want to make it.

(Pause.)

ELAINE: I suppose…I suppose you could have a point.

JOY: Could? Of course I do. Just because Stephen doesn't like sushi doesn't mean I can't drop into Mr. Takimoto's and nibble on his uni once in a while, does it?

ELAINE: Well…yes, but–

JOY: Anyway, Graham's opened the door; the rest is up to you. Only, if you choose to do nothing, for God's sake stop moaning on at me about it – I've enough on my plate.

(Pause.)

ELAINE: I'm not sure what I shall do. I need time to think…I think. But I will admit that you've forced me to look at things from a…a different perspective…one I hadn't considered. And I am grateful for it, Joy – really I am. And I know you think that I dislike you underneath, because you were always the pretty one and I was always second best, but I don't…I don't, Joy. I've never begrudged you that. Even though you were cruel sometimes. And your opinions really do mean a lot to me…and I promise I shall give them very serious consideration.

JOY: Haven't a clue what you're talking about, but as far as the last part's concerned – good.

ELAINE: And, God forbid, if Graham should ever have a similar dream, then I…well, I shall… definitely take decisive measures.

(Beat.)

JOY: What?

ELAINE: I said, I shall take decisive measures.

JOY: Did you say, "Dream"?

ELAINE: Yes.

JOY: What dream?

ELAINE: Graham's dream – about having sex with another man.

JOY: (*Incredulous.*) It was a dream?

ELAINE: Yes. (*Beat.*) Did I not mention that?

JOY: (*Furious.*) No! No, you bloody well didn't!

ELAINE: Oh…well, it was.

JOY: For Christ's sake! You mean I scrambled over here like a bat out of hell, after a day of sheer bloody torture, thinking you were on the edge of an abyss, all because of some stupid bloody dream?

ELAINE: I'm sorry, I…I found it very disturbing.

JOY: You're the one that's disturbed, if you ask me! For God's sake, the man has a subconscious fantasy about sex with another man and you start flailing around like some demented octopus! Christ, I hate you sometimes, I *really* do!

ELAINE: Joy, he performed acts upon him…he told me.

JOY: So-bloody-what?

ELAINE: He allowed this young man to…to enter him!

JOY: *It was a dream!*

ELAINE: He enjoyed it!

JOY: (*Standing.*) All right, that's it – I've had enough. I'm sorry, Elaine, but Stephen's brats and middle-class hysteria all in one day, it's…it's just too much. I'm leaving.

(*JOY crosses to the door L.*)

ELAINE: (*Beseechingly.*) Oh, Joy! Joy!

JOY: (*Turning in the doorway.*) No, Elaine. No! I have just imparted very personal details and aspects regarding my private life to you because, as your sister, I felt a duty and an obligation to do so, since you'd led me to believe that you were in a strange place and needed guidance. As it turns out, you're insane and I'm a fool, so let's just cut our losses. Good afternoon.

(*JOY exits. ELAINE hurries to the doorway and calls after her.*)

ELAINE: But what about me? What about my private life? Why does everything always have to happen to someone else?

(*The front door is heard slamming. ELAINE turns and leans against the doorjamb. Pause.*)

ELAINE: (*Dejectedly.*) Why can't I be someone else?

(*The lights fade to BLACK.*)

Scene 3

Early afternoon, the following day. The kitchen is deserted. Momentarily, a doorbell is heard, followed by the sound of someone descending a staircase. The front door is heard opening.

ELAINE: (*Off.*) Yes?

MAN: (*Off.*) U-Bend-We Mend.

ELAINE: (*Off.*) What?

MAN: (*Off.*) U-Bend-We Mend.

ELAINE: (*Off.*) What are you talking about?

MAN: (*Off.*) You're plugged up.

ELAINE: (*Off.*) I'm what?

MAN: (*Off.*) Plugged up. Least, you said you were…'ang on. (*The sounds of buttons being pushed on an electronic device are heard.*) Yep, 'ere you are. Got a call from a Mr…Wavering, sayin' you was plugged up. It's right 'ere – the address and everything.

  (*Beat.*)

ELAINE: (*Off.*) Oh! Oh, God yes, the sink – the waste disposal. Yes, yes, yes, come in, come in…this way.

  (*ELAINE enters, followed by a rather handsome young man in his early twenties, wearing a baseball cap, jeans, and a tee shirt with the logo "U-Bend-We Mend" emblazoned on the back.*)

31

ELAINE: (*Pointing at the sink.*) Um…it's here, the problem's here.

MAN: In the sink?

ELAINE: Yes, exactly.

MAN: (*As he places his clipboard and paraphernalia on the kitchen table.*) Good…that's good, that is. Makes my job a lot easier when I'm dealin' with someone who knows a bit about what they're talkin' about.

ELAINE: Yes, I'd imagine.

MAN: So what did you do?

ELAINE: I'm sorry?

MAN: What did ya shove down it? Tea bags? Banana skins? Potato peelin's?

ELAINE: Nothing. I didn't do anything. It just stopped working.

MAN: (*Speculatively.*) Right…right, right, right. Yep…yep, I've seen this many, many times before.

ELAINE: Have you?

MAN: Oh, yeah. "It just stopped workin'"…very common.

ELAINE: Is it?

MAN: Yep. Happens all the time.

ELAINE: I mean, I just turned it on and it started making this horrible noise.

MAN: What kind of noise?

ELAINE: I don't know, just some sort of grinding noise.

MAN: A grinding noise?

ELAINE: Yes, exactly.

MAN: Oh dear.

ELAINE: Is that bad?

MAN: It might be. Let's have a look.

(*The MAN bends over and opens the doors beneath the sink, his perfectly rounded buttocks protruding upwards, which ELAINE cannot stop herself from admiring.*)

MAN: Ahhh…

ELAINE: (*Instinctively.*) Yes.

MAN: What?

ELAINE: What?

MAN: It's your u-bend.

ELAINE: Is it?

MAN: No question.

ELAINE: What's wrong with it?

MAN: Well, it looks normal enough on the outside – nice and smooth and well-rounded. See those curves?

ELAINE: (*Leaning a little closer.*) Yes…yes, I see them.

MAN: But I can tell – almost without lookin' – that it's clogged up.

ELAINE: So…what should we do?

(*The MAN stands and looks ELAINE squarely in the face.*)

MAN: It needs a good probin'.

(*Beat.*)

ELAINE: Does it?

MAN: Oh, yeah. If ever I saw a tube that needed a good probin', it's yours. 'Ang on, let me switch you off at your mains so we can get a better look.

(*The MAN dives down beneath the sink once more, as ELAINE continues, in spite of her modesty, to indulge her eyes on the sight of his behind.*)

ELAINE: You, um…you certainly seem to have a firm…grasp of things.

MAN: Darlin', puttin' your pipes in my hands is one of the best decisions you ever made. Now, let's just prize this loose so I can 'ave a good look.

(The MAN continues to tinker some more, as ELAINE vainly attempts to resist her impulse to stare.)

MAN: Oh…oh, Jesus!

ELAINE: What?

MAN: This is unbelievable!

ELAINE: What is?

MAN: Christ, this must've been cloggin' up for years. I'm surprised it's taken you this long to ask for help.

ELAINE: Is it that bad?

MAN: It's very bad.

ELAINE: How bad?

MAN: Very, *very* bad.

ELAINE: What should we do?

MAN: The only thing we can do.

ELAINE: What's that?

(Again the MAN stands and faces ELAINE in a very deliberate manner.)

MAN: Like I said, give it a good probin'.

(Beat.)

ELAINE: And…how do we do that?

MAN: (*His tone ever more insinuating.*) Well, that's where my expertise comes in, don't it?

ELAINE: Does it?

MAN: Oh, yeah. I think if we take it step by step we'll have you opened up in no time.

ELAINE: Yes…yes, good.

MAN: But it's gonna need to be a team effort. I'll need you to work with me on this.

ELAINE: Whatever you say.

MAN: Good. Now, this won't be an easy job. There's a lot of build up in there, and with that much build up it sometimes gets a bit messy.

ELAINE: Does it?

MAN: Sometimes. But it don't need to…all depends on how you handle it.

ELAINE: I see.

MAN: But if we just handle it professionally – in, out, pay the bill, end of story – everyone's happy, right?

(*Beat.*)

ELAINE: Right.

MAN: And if I'm gonna do this job right, then that means I gotta use my special tool, and that means I'm gonna need you to be there to help me. (*Beat.*) And I think you know what that means, don't you?

(*Beat.*)

ELAINE: (*Conspiratorially.*) Yes, I…I think I do.

MAN: Good.

(*With his back to the fourth wall, the MAN proceeds to unzip his jeans and pull out his penis.*)

MAN: Right then, playtime's over – let's get to work.

ELAINE: (*Taken aback by his forthrightness.*) What…what are you doing?

MAN: I told ya – if we're gonna fix this, it's gonna need my special tool.

ELAINE: And…and that's it, is it?

MAN: They don't come more special than this, love, trust me.

ELAINE: Yes, I…I – I, I can see that.

MAN: Well?

ELAINE: What, um…what…what should I do?

MAN: For right now, I just need you to hold it.

ELAINE: Hold it?

MAN: Yeah, while I work out the logistics.

ELAINE: Of course, yes…um…

(*ELAINE places her hand around the MAN'S penis.*)

ELAINE: Like this?

MAN: (*With a sigh of gratification.*) Yeah, just like that.

(*Pause.*)

ELAINE: Now what?

MAN: Now, I need you to…

(*The MAN suddenly hoists ELAINE'S skirt, pulls down her underwear and lifts her onto the front ledge of the kitchen sink.*)

MAN: …let me take a good look at the problem.

ELAINE: Ow!…um, yes…yes, I think you should.

(*The MAN buries his head in ELAINE'S crotch for a brief period, which is soon accompanied by various exclamations of satisfaction from ELAINE. Momentarily he re-emerges.*)

MAN: Just what I thought.

ELAINE: Is it?

MAN: All right – 'ere we go.

(The MAN inserts himself into ELAINE.)

ELAINE: Oh!

MAN: Easy does it.

ELAINE: Oh!

MAN: Relax.

ELAINE: Oh, yes!

MAN: That's it.

ELAINE: Oh, Christ!

MAN: That's me.

ELAINE: Keep going.

MAN: I intend to.

ELAINE: Don't stop!

MAN: I haven't started.

ELAINE: Oh, God!

MAN: I'm workin' on it.

(ELAINE'S moans become ever more fervent as the MAN continues his thrusting.)

ELAINE: God, I'd forgotten…oh…

(*In her fervor, ELAINE accidentally knocks over a pile of plates and saucers into the sink, creating a loud cacophony of clattering dishes.*)

MAN: I've got ya.

ELAINE: Yes!

MAN: Who's ya daddy?

ELAINE: What?

MAN: Who's ya daddy?

MAN: Well, it was…um…his…uh…Kenneth

MAN: Who's ya daddy?

ELAINE: Kenneth!

MAN: (*Insistently.*) Who's ya daddy?

ELAINE: It's–

MAN: I'm ya daddy!

ELAINE: Oh, yes…yes, of course!

MAN: Who's ya daddy?

ELAINE: You are.

MAN: Who's ya daddy?

ELAINE: You're my daddy.

MAN: Who's ya daddy?

ELAINE: You're my daddy.

MAN: Who?

ELAINE: You.

MAN: Who?

ELAINE: You.

MAN: Who?

ELAINE: You.

MAN: Ah...ah...ahhh... (*Beat.*) Ohhh...

(*Pause.*)

ELAINE: Have we...are we...have we finished?

MAN: (*As he withdraws from her.*) Well, I have, love – can't speak for you.

ELAINE: Right. Right, yes...yes, of course.

(*The MAN zips up his jeans as ELAINE climbs down from the sink.*)

ELAINE: Do you, um...well, thank you...thank you...

MAN: The name's—

ELAINE: (*Hurriedly raising her hand in opposition.*) No! I don't want to know!

MAN: Please yourself.

> (*The MAN slides back under the sink and continues with his work. ELAINE looks around the kitchen with a faint air of panic in her expression. She suddenly begins to tidy and straighten various objects around the kitchen, as if to reestablish a sense of normalcy. As her actions becoming ever more manic, she instinctively grabs a glass of water from the countertop and empties it into the sink.*)

MAN: (*From under the sink.*) Shit!

ELAINE: Oh, my God! Oh God, I'm so sorry – I completely forgot!

MAN: (*Loudly.*) Man at work!

ELAINE: Yes.

> (*ELAINE sits at one of the chairs and stares out ahead, looking completely bewildered. Soon after, the MAN reappears from beneath the sink.*)

MAN: Right then, I'm off.

ELAINE: (*Standing.*) That was very…you're very…is it fixed?

MAN: Oh, it's fixed all right. When I'm on the job I get very few complaints, believe you me.

ELAINE: No, I…I don't doubt it.

(*The MAN takes his clipboard from the table and hands it to ELAINE.*)

MAN: Now, if you'll just sign at the bottom, that'll be forty quid.

ELAINE: (*As she's signing.*) Gosh, is that all?

MAN: (*Pointing to the small print on his tee shirt.*) That's U-Bend-We Mend, darlin' – "We plumb for love, not money."

ELAINE: (*As she reaches into her purse.*) Apparently so. (*Handing him the cash.*) Well, thank you…very much…for, um…everything.

MAN: (*Gathering his things.*) Don't mention it, love. Like my old Gran used to say, "Share your love, son, don't share a needle."

ELAINE: (*A little surprised.*) Your grandmother said that?

MAN: (*As he starts towards the door L.*) Yeah. (*Stopping, scratching his head.*) No, 'ang on, that weren't her. Who the hell was it then? (*Beat.*) No, no, no, that's right, it weren't me Gran – may she rest in peace – it was Phil…may he rest in peace.

ELAINE: Ah…a friend?

MAN: Yeah. No. Well, not a friend really…me old supplier.

ELAINE: Supplier?

MAN: Dealer.

ELAINE: Dealer? You mean… drugs?

MAN: Well, it weren't fine art, darlin' – not in Harlseden.

ELAINE: Oh.

MAN: Poor old Phil.

(*Beat.*)

ELAINE: And did you?

MAN: What?

ELAINE: Share a needle.

MAN: No, 'course not. Hardly ever.

ELAINE: What do you mean, "Hardly ever"?

MAN: Like I say, virtually never.

ELAINE: So you did?

MAN: Well…once or twice at most – but only with Phil.

ELAINE: And what became of this…Phil?

MAN: Dead…AIDS, poor bugger. (*Looking skyward.*) Now he's upon high…pushin' it just a little bit higher…makin' them angelic smiles just a little bit wider, God bless him.

ELAINE: (*Increasingly agitated.*) But…but don't you know that…I mean, you could be…I mean, for God's sake, you might…

MAN: Might, might, maybe tonight. Look, love, that was then –

this is now. I had a problem – I got it sorted out. Now I'm clean, I got myself a decent job, and I'm only looking forward, not back.

ELAINE: (*With evident alarm.*): But, haven't you thought about…I mean…

MAN: I'm not the type, love – not me. We're a tough breed, my family – strong as horses. It's in our blood.

ELAINE: Nevertheless…

MAN: Just go with the flow, darlin' – it's all you can do. And if your flow gets backed up, well…you know the number. (*As he exits.*) Ta'ta!

> (*ELAINE remains motionless, trying to absorb what has just occurred. The sound of the front door shutting interrupts her abstraction. Moving downstage C., she holds out her left arm and stares for some time at the vascular map of her blood vessels.*)

ELAINE: (*Quietly and almost without expression.*) Shit.

> (*The lights slowly fade to BLACK.*)

ACT II

Scene 1

Approximately two weeks later. JOY is found sitting at the kitchen table looking utterly bored. ELAINE'S voice is heard off-stage, evidently finishing up a telephone conversation. Presently, ELAINE enters through the door L.

ELAINE: (*Sheepishly.*) Sorry about that.

JOY: Mmm.

ELAINE: That was Graham – wanted to let me know he's working late tonight.

JOY: Mmm.

ELAINE: It's so good of you to come, Joy.

JOY: Yes, it is.

ELAINE: I know how valuable your time is.

JOY: I'm not convinced that you do, but I will say this: if you've dragged me over here on another wild goose chase of cockeyed hysteria then it'll be the last time you do. I'm sure you're familiar with the tale of the bored housewife that cried wolf.

ELAINE: Can I get you something? A cup of tea, perhaps?

JOY: Elaine, I don't have time.

ELAINE: Coffee?

JOY: (*Impatiently.*) *Elaine.*

ELAINE: A drink?

JOY: What do you have?

ELAINE: Well…there's half a bottle of Chardonnay in the fridge.

JOY: God, how crushingly predictable. All right, make it quick.

> (*ELAINE fetches the wine from the refrigerator and a glass from one of the cabinets.*)

ELAINE: It's really rather good. Graham and I experimented with it the other night. It's from this new little boutique winery that a good friend of Graham's has part-ownership in.

JOY: (*Apathetically.*) Fascinating.

ELAINE: (*As she pours.*) Graham thinks there's a tad too much cedar in the aftertaste, but I find it quite aromatic. Almost woodsy, if that didn't sound so…I don't know…rural.

JOY: As long as it's boozy, darling, I really don't care. Aren't you having one?

ELAINE: Oh, I can't drink in the afternoon – gives me a thumping headache.

JOY: Gives me a thumping headache if I don't. Anyway, I can't stay long.

ELAINE: I know, I know.

JOY: Well then – out with it.

ELAINE: (*With a sigh.*) I…I don't quite know how to tell you…not in a way that makes any sense. It still doesn't make sense to me, really. But the fact is, I…Joy, I–

JOY: (*Having taken a sip from her wine.*) Urgh! Good God! Woodsy? This tastes like tree sap!

ELAINE: But wait…wait for the aftertaste.

(*Beat.*)

JOY: With a hint of…Dutch elm disease.

ELAINE: Well, I'm…I'm sure there's something else. I can check if you like.

JOY: No, no, I'm sure I'll get accustomed to it – or over it. Go on.

(*Beat.*)

ELAINE: Well, you see I…I've made a mistake.

JOY: Yes.

ELAINE: A dreadful, dreadful mistake. One that I am now paying *very* dearly for.

JOY: Well, I told you that on your wedding day – you should've listened.

ELAINE: I'm being serious.

JOY: So am I.

ELAINE: (*In a sudden outburst.*) Joy, I had sex!

JOY: You what?

ELAINE: I did it. Can you believe it? I actually did it!

JOY: Well, it's not that hard, darling – they don't give you a certificate or anything, you know.

ELAINE: (*In hushed tones.*) With…with someone else…I cheated – no, not cheated, I…however you put it the other day…that's what I did.

JOY: You did not!

ELAINE: I did, I swear!

JOY: (*Impressed.*) Well, well. Well done, darling. I'd all but given up on you. I hope it was someone yummy.

(*Beat.*)

ELAINE: No. No, not…not yummy. (*Upon reflection.*) Well, I suppose he was rather yummy, actually…at the time. Rather young and yummy.

JOY: Ooh, I'm almost envious of you – there's a first.

ELAINE: But…afterwards – after the yumminess – it left rather a bitter taste.

49

JOY: (*After taking another swig from her glass.*) Oh, don't worry about the aftertaste, darling, as long as it hits the spot.

ELAINE: That's just it – I've a horrible feeling it did.

(*JOY finishes the last of her wine and stands as if to leave.*)

JOY: Wonderful! Well, congratulations, darling – must dash.

ELAINE: No!

JOY: What?

ELAINE: You can't go.

JOY: Why not?

ELAINE: I haven't finished.

JOY: Darling, I don't need to know the sordid details – I do have a sordid life of my own, you know.

ELAINE: But I haven't finished – I haven't told you.

JOY: Told me what?

(*Pause.*)

ELAINE: Joy, I…I think I might be dying.

JOY: (*Rolling her eyes.*) We're all dying, darling – it's all finite…thank Christ.

ELAINE: No, I mean I think I'm *dying* dying…because of him.

JOY: Don't tell me you've become smitten over some gangly youth. For God's sake, Elaine, you can't get involved with them – it's just sex.

ELAINE: Joy, he…God, I feel so stupid, but I…this young man was…

JOY: What?

ELAINE: He was…

JOY: *What?*

ELAINE: You see, he'd–

(*Suddenly the sound of JOY'S cellular phone ringing is heard.*)

JOY: Shit! (*She reaches into her handbag and retrieves a very petite mobile phone. She holds the phone before her so as to identify the caller.*) Urgh! (*With irritation in her voice she answers the call.*) What?…So?…No, I cannot!…Because I'm at my sister's…Elaine…*Elaine!*…The one with the eyebrows…Then you'll just have to take them to the golf course with you, won't you?…Then shout at them, like I do…Look, it was your decision to breed with that harpy – they're not my spawn; you deal with them…Well, I don't know – can't you palm them off onto Barb and Tim?…Well, then you have a clear choice, don't you? You can sacrifice the game of golf, or you can sacrifice your brats – preferably in a way that won't stain the carpet! (*She abruptly hangs up the phone.*) Sorry, darling, you were saying?

(*Beat.*)

ELAINE: I don't know what I'm saying, really – or how to say it.

(*Beat.*) This is one of those times in my life where I want to collect all of my thoughts together and put them into neat little piles, all labeled and clearly marked, so that I can make sensible, practical decisions. But I can't. They all keep whizzing around in my head, never staying still long enough for me to grab hold of them.

JOY: Well try to grab a few, darling, because I have no idea what you're talking about.

ELAINE: All right...all right, I shall. (*Taking a deep breath.*) He – this young man – was a recovering drug addict and we had very rough and very unprotected sex. And later...when I went to the bathroom...there was blood.

JOY: (*Scoffing.*) What? What sensationalist claptrap! (*Beat.*) Is this one of your pathetic "Elaine" attempts at shocking me? Well, I'm sorry darling, but you've failed – yet again.

ELAINE: And now I'm not sure what I've done.

JOY: Elaine, it takes more than a borrowed plot line from EastEnders to pull the wool over my eyes. So I take it there was no yummy young man, and this was all some desperately sad attempt to impress me?

ELAINE: No!

JOY: God, I'm such a fool.

ELAINE: It's the truth!

JOY: You did it again.

ELAINE: Joy!

ELAINE: Well, you may not have many talents, Elaine, but I'll tell you this much: you certainly are adept at making me look like a complete and utter idiot. Congratulations, darling – well done!

ELAINE: (*Pleading.*) Joy, *please*, for God's sake, I don't know how else to tell you. A young man came here to fix the waste disposal, I let him in, he went to work, and before I knew what was happening we were having sex. And I was enjoying it, and I didn't care about the consequences because I just wanted it to happen, and because it felt good, and…but I… (*Her voice cracking.*) I didn't know.

(*Pause.*)

JOY: Good God, I almost think you're serious.

ELAINE: Of course I am; I told you I am.

JOY: You mean you had sex here – in this kitchen?

ELAINE: Yes. (*Pointing at the sink.*) Right there.

JOY: (*Astonished.*) By the sink?

ELAINE: On it.

(*Beat. JOY stares at ELAINE for a moment in incredulity.*)

JOY: Don't think me slow, darling, but…let me just make sure I've got this right: You let a…a plumber – a complete stranger – into your home and proceeded to have sexual intercourse with him whilst perched upon your kitchen sink?

ELAINE: Yes.

JOY: But...what on earth took possession of you?

ELAINE: Nothing, that's the point. I wasn't thinking. It wasn't preplanned. I didn't expect, or want, or anticipate anything – aside from the waste disposal working again. It just happened. I don't know how, he just had this way about him that was...there...just there – obvious and straightforward and uncomplicated, and...and sexual. And I...I went with it, because...because I wanted to, and because it was so easy to because he made it easy, and because...because I'm so sick and tired of being whatever it is that I am all the bloody time – stuck in here like some obligatory bowl of fruit that nobody actually wants to eat. I just didn't want to be me for once...just once.

(*Beat.*)

JOY: Well, I can sympathize with that, darling, but honestly...on the sink...with the plumber.

ELAINE: It was your idea.

JOY: (*Aghast.*) I beg your pardon? It most certainly was not!

ELAINE: You said I should open myself up more...look for other avenues.

JOY: Yes, but there are avenues, darling, and there are...well, quite frankly, alleyways.

ELAINE: There's no need to be so haughty about it.

JOY: Or perhaps I should say gutters?

ELAINE: I don't see that there's any difference.

JOY: Elaine, there is a world of difference. I only ever have sex with friends of Stephen's – or trusted acquaintances at the very least – and even then only the married ones. And it's *always* in the room of a highly reputable hotel. I mean, my God, how else could one maintain one's self-respect?

ELAINE: But it's all just sex. Sex is sex, isn't it?

JOY: Of course it isn't, darling, it's like everything else – it all has a pedigree. That's like saying shoes are just shoes…though from what I generally see you plodding around in that argument's hardly likely to carry much weight. (*Beat.*) But anyway, didn't you think of Graham?

ELAINE: (*Rather adamantly.*) No. For once in this wretched life I thought of no one but me.

JOY: But what about his comfort level with this, Elaine?

ELAINE: What "comfort level"?

JOY: Not that, God forbid, he should ever know about it, but…well, it does happen. And if that were the case, I think you'd have an obligation to offer some small token of solace, don't you? I mean, if you'd slipped off for the afternoon to some cozy little B & B with one of Graham's attractive business partners – married, of course – for a little rumpy-pumpy on the pretense of attending a grief-stricken niece, say…well, it all has a nice veneer that everyone can live with. But honestly, Elaine, banging the plumber perched amongst last night's dirty dishes, well…that's a very big pill to swallow – even for someone as hapless as Graham.

ELAINE: But I told you, I didn't plan it that way – it just happened. Out of the blue I was suddenly presented with a clear, unobstructed opportunity not to be Elaine Wavering and I went with it. Was it classy or sophisticated? No. Will I mention it in my Christmas update letter to friends and family? Probably not. Did I enjoy it? Yes I did. And now I shall pay for it…with my life.

JOY: Oh, don't be so bloody melodramatic.

ELAINE: If only I were.

JOY: All right, so you had a quickie with the plumber – it's not the end of the world. It could've been the milkman.

ELAINE: The plumber who was a former drug addict.

JOY: (*Rolling her eyes.*) Yes, I remember. And they say the age of romance is dead.

ELAINE: Whose drug supplier died of AIDS.

JOY: Like I say. (*Beat.*) Why are you looking at me like that? So?

ELAINE: With whom he'd shared syringes with on more than one occasion.

JOY: Oh. (*Beat.*) *Oh.*

ELAINE: Yes.

JOY: Oh God, and… (*Beat.*) And you…

ELAINE: I told you.

JOY: Yes…without protection.

ELAINE: Yes.

JOY: Yes.

ELAINE: So you see…

JOY: Yes.

ELAINE: And now I…

(Pause.)

JOY: Oh, you bloody fool!

ELAINE: Joy…please don't be angry with me. I…I just don't think I'm up to it.

JOY: (Angrily.) I'm not angry with you; I just can't understand how you could be so… (Beat. Pushing her glass forward.) I need more.

ELAINE: I thought you didn't like it?

JOY: I don't.

ELAINE: Right.

(ELAINE fetches another bottle of the wine from a cabinet and proceeds to uncork it.)

JOY: Look, let me just say right now that I am not about to lecture you about things that you, as an informed adult, should already be patently aware of – i.e. that in this day and age you simply cannot go around having unprotected sex with anyone, anywhere, whenever you feel like it; not just because of the risk of HIV infection, which is, of course, by far the most serious, but for a whole host of other unsavoury social calling cards, such as hepatitis, gonorrhea, herpes and crabs, to name but a few; but also because, even at your age, Elaine, you cannot rule out the possibility of pregnancy, because I remember reading some story recently where this French woman conceived at the age of 97, or something hideous like that, and even though it was all done with test tubes and lasers and things, the fact is you're not 97 and stranger things have happened; but more to the point, I desperately hope that you're not one of those troglodytes that still likes to believe that HIV and AIDS are the sole realm of homosexuals and sub-Saharan Africans, because if you are, you're not only an idiot, you're one of those lamentable and all-too-common bi-products of the so-called "information age" that only ever reads the "informative headline," never the full story. So…rather than lecture you, I will simply say this: What are you doing about it?

ELAINE: (*Somewhat taken aback.*) Joy, I…I never knew you were so…

JOY: So what?

ELAINE: I don't know.

>	(*ELAINE at last pours the wine, having fetched a glass for herself also.*)

JOY: Elaine, I have no idea what you think I am or am not, quite frankly. How could I? It's not as if we were ever really that close. Impossible really, since you were always the favourite. But I've always lived my life on the principal of knowing what I'm talking about. And so I do. Nothing happens in the world of misses and petite's formal and eveningwear fashions that I don't know about, and that's how I survive – professionally. I also happen to have sexual intercourse on a semi-regular basis with people I don't know particularly well – not as well as Stephen, at least – and so I keep myself informed on the potential pleasures and pitfalls thereof, and that is also how I survive – physically. It's not smart, it's just common sense.

ELAINE: (*After taking a sip from her wine.*) I don't know why, but…but whenever you talk about yourself you always seem to make me feel…so much less. Less than what I try to make myself believe that I actually am, at least. I don't think that it's intended, but…it's always there – underneath.

JOY: Well, that's probably because I'm a far more interesting and well-rounded individual than you are, Elaine. Hard to hear, I know, darling, but there it is.

ELAINE: Exactly. I always feel as though I have to prove myself – without ever quite knowing how to do it.

JOY: I wasn't being serious.

ELAINE: I know you weren't – although sometimes I'm not sure when you are and when you aren't – but I was.

JOY: Oh, what rubbish! You've never had to prove anything. You were always the golden child and you know it.

ELAINE: I was not.

JOY: Of course you were.

ELAINE: I wasn't – I just did what was expected of me, that's all.

JOY: Yes, and I didn't, and I paid the price, so fuck them – both of them…may they rest in peace.

ELAINE: Joy!

JOY: Joy what?

ELAINE: They were your parents!

JOY: Elaine, you are referring to the science of biology; I am referring to voluntary acts of love and caring, and the truth is they never contributed one single ounce toward my emotional well-being or self-esteem when they were alive, so why the hell should I honour them now that they're dead? So, with all due respect and what have you – fuck them!

ELAINE: How can you talk like that?

JOY: Because it's the truth and you know damned well it is.

ELAINE: But you never needed their help. You were always the clever one, the pretty one, the independent one, the one who excelled at *everything*. You were standing on your own two feet before you were born. The only reason they lavished attention on me was because I needed it.

JOY: And I didn't.

ELAINE: No. You had success written all over you from the outset – you and Fiona both – it was obvious to anyone. All that was written about me was the same depressing words in my report book every year: "Could try harder."

JOY: Then why didn't you?

ELAINE: I couldn't, that was all I had – and they knew it. They did their best to encourage me, but…I knew that they knew that deep down inside it was hopeless; that I was marriage material at best.

JOY: (*Caustically*.) They gave you self-worth, Elaine.

ELAINE: They didn't. They tried…and still then you were the one that ended up with it.

JOY: (*Staring into her glass*.) News to me. At any rate, at least they acknowledged you…made you feel like you mattered.

ELAINE: I was acknowledged only because I was a liability – a potential embarrassment to them.

JOY: It was attention, wasn't it? What more do you want?

ELAINE: It wasn't real attention, Joy. It wasn't love either. It was an ongoing salvage operation on a child they feared would never amount to anything – which, of course, was true. I suppose I should at least take some pride in having lived down to their expectations.

JOY: Christ, darling, must you really be so self-loathing? It's a very unattractive indulgence – even in a woman.

ELAINE: No, it's not that…it's not, really. I don't hate *me*…that person I started out as…that I still am, deep down inside. I just hate what I've become…which is, in essence, the same thing, I suppose. And I think that's it really – I haven't changed. I haven't progressed. I thought time would produce a newer, improved version of me, but it hasn't…it's still the same old me in the same package…just older and tattier. And to cap it all, I think I just contradicted myself.

(*Pause.*)

JOY: How strange. I always thought that you were so…you seemed so…oblivious to everything. (*Beat.*) Why did you never speak up? There's a chance I'd have listened. Perhaps we might even have been a little…a bit closer…you never know.

ELAINE: Because for one thing, we never really talk, do we? On the rare occasions we do get together we just…say things at each other. And for another, it's awfully hard admitting to yourself, let alone anyone else, that you are, and always have been, an unmitigated failure.

JOY: What on earth do you mean? Just because you don't have children or a career doesn't mean you're a failure. I mean, look at me. I don't have children, I simply inherited two lamentable attempts at holding a marriage together. And as far as my career is concerned…well, in all honesty, it's about as fulfilling as a lukewarm Chinese takeaway on a wet Tuesday evening. But I would never consider myself a failure. I see myself as someone who's made the best they could with the cards they were dealt.

ELAINE: But that's you.

JOY: Yes, it is. And you're you. You can just be *you*, you know – there's no law against it.

ELAINE: But don't you understand? – I've been trying very hard to be me all my life…and I still don't know how to do it.

JOY: Well, if it's any consolation, I've spent my entire life trying to be anyone other *than* me, and I think the end result is more or less the same. If I ever am me again, I'll give you a more definitive opinion. (*Pause.*) Odd, isn't it? You think you see something for what it is, when in actuality you may have absolutely no idea of what you're looking at. (*Beat.*) Hard to believe as I look at you now that I was once so horribly jealous of you.

ELAINE: (*Astounded.*) Of me?

JOY: Yes – can you imagine? It's almost embarrassing. And not just because you were the favourite – though, God knows, that was bad enough – but because you were always so bloody proper and good and…*pure.* God, how I envied that purity. Probably because I knew I could never have it. In fact, I think I'd already lost it by the time I started thinking about it. I threw my hat into the ring at a *very* early age, Elaine.

ELAINE: I never had a choice, really. No one ever seemed to find me that attractive in order to give me one.

JOY: (*Wistfully.*) Oh, how I admired that unsoiled virtue. So saintly and wholesome and…well…*nice.* (*Beat.*) Of course, after your little indoor plumbing job, there's another idealistic vision gone down the toilet…or sink, in your case.

ELAINE: I think I must be fated…I take just one tiny little bite of forbidden fruit and I still manage to make a complete balls up of it.

JOY: Darling, you didn't balls it up, you just acted rashly. But in this irrational world of ours you simply can't afford to do that – the stakes are too high; there's too many risks.

ELAINE: Risks? I don't know risks. I don't understand them. They've never been a part of my life. I just did one thing, one time – *one time* – and now I must pay for it with this. It's not fair, Joy, it's not. I don't care what you say, there's no justification for it. It's as if life was sitting there, waiting to ambush me, waiting for me to step out of line, to step outside of my little boundaries, and then...wham! And for what? Desire for another person – to *feel* another person. To connect. To feel connected to someone...*something*. For Christ's sake, Joy, at the end of the day I'm just like everyone else. And the most ridiculous part, if you want to know the honest truth, is the sex wasn't even that good – not really. But I'll tell you what did feel good: I felt wanted. I felt wanted by somebody...and that felt very good – even under those coarse, crude circumstances. And I haven't felt that in a long, long time, and...and...and that's all I can say. (*Beat. Her eyes beginning to well up.*) Except that...that...that I think everyone needs to feel that sometimes...wanted...for whatever reason. Just to remind them that...that they're someone...that they matter...even if it's only for a couple of minutes with a stranger who doesn't really care anyway...and that...that shouldn't be a bad thing...that's all. (*Beat.*) That's all.

(*ELAINE bursts into tears. JOY moves next to her and holds her in her arms.*)

JOY: Oh, Elaine, please...please don't cry...please don't. Don't make me do it.

ELAINE (*Through her sobs.*) I'm sorry...I'm trying not to. (*Beat.*) But it's...I think it's good to cry sometimes – lets it all out.

JOY: No it's not. Not for me.

ELAINE: I think so…even for you.

JOY: (*With a tremor in her voice.*) It isn't and I don't intend to do it. It's something I promised myself in 1987 that I would never ever do again.

ELAINE: Why…what happened in 1987?

JOY: I don't wish to discuss it.

ELAINE: No, Joy, please. Tell me. I'd like to know. (*Beat.*) I want to know

JOY: (*Tentatively.*) Oh, but…no, you'll think it facile.

(*ELAINE looks at her imploringly. JOY finally relents with a sigh.*)

JOY: All right. But I did warn you. (*Beat.*) I read an article in Marie Claire that described the ravaging dermatological effects of excessive facial contortions, such as frowning, smiling…and especially crying. And in that moment I realized the very real and very heavy price to be paid for outward displays of emotion. And I promised myself on that day that, however upsetting the situation, all of my crying henceforth would be done…internally…because… (*Her voice beginning to crack.*) Because I saw no sense in making two tragedies from one, and now… (*As she begins to weep.*) Now I shall look old before my time…just like you. I'm sorry, darling, but it has to be said, and there it is. It may sound ridiculous to you, but…but it's my currency, for God's sake.

ELAINE: What is?

JOY: (*Pointing to her face.*) This. Whatever it is that I've achieved in this life has been largely due to this. What's inside is nothing special – ten a penny, really – but this…this opens doors. And I know that must sound grotesquely superficial, but that's the way it is and it's all I have…and…and I'm terrified of losing it.

ELAINE: (*Embracing her sister.*) It doesn't matter, it really doesn't. (*Beat.*) Joy, I do love you, you know – you do know that?

JOY: (*Wiping her eyes with her hand.*) I suppose…and I suppose I love you too, Elaine…in an…odd sort of way. Hadn't really given it much thought.

(*They continue to embrace for a moment or two before JOY pulls away.*)

JOY: Yes, well…that's enough. I'd say, wouldn't you? I…I think you've got the…general sense of my feelings. Haven't you?

(*ELAINE nods.*)

JOY: I'm sorry, darling, but I'm…I'm just not very good at this sort of thing. Never have been. Hereditary, I suppose.

ELAINE: You don't have to explain.

JOY: I just don't want to get all morbid and gloomy about it all – not if it's not necessary. (*Taking a deep breath.*) So, let's be positive. Although, in retrospect, I suppose I could've phrased that better. But anyway, I…I go back to my original question: What are you doing about it?

ELAINE: Crossing my fingers.

JOY: (*Rolling her eyes.*) Oh, well done, darling – that was quick thinking. I mean on a realistic, practical level?

ELAINE: I…I had some blood tests done.

JOY: Where?

ELAINE: At a clinic.

JOY: What clinic?

ELAINE: A clinic where they do blood tests.

JOY: And?

ELAINE: They tested my blood.

JOY: And?

ELAINE: And they called this morning with the results.

JOY: Oh, for Christ's sake, Elaine…*and?*

ELAINE: And they were negative.

(*Beat.*)

JOY: Ohh… (*Clasping her hands to her face.*) Oh, thank God.

ELAINE: But…that doesn't really mean anything.

JOY: What do you mean? Of course it does – it means that you tested negative.

ELAINE: I have to go back for more tests in six months. Nothing's certain until then. Apparently, it can take some time before the virus makes its presence known. I'd have thought you'd have known that, you being so informed about everything.

JOY: Well, I...I can't keep track of everything, darling. And let's face it, HIV infection is so 'yesterday's news' nowadays. (*Beat.*) Oh, this is ridiculous. I don't like this, Elaine; I don't like it at all.

ELAINE: Maybe not, but...well...there it is.

JOY: So...what now?

ELAINE: Now I wait.

JOY: Wait? But how can you, for God's sake? Your life is in the balance.

ELAINE: Yes...yes it is. And I've weighing it up. For the first time in my life I'm in a position where I'm able to see the whole thing for what it is...naked...stripped of all its cozy little self-deceptions. As a result of a few minutes illicit pleasure with the local plumber, I can now see what it is that I've been hauling around all these years. It's all on exhibition – just for me. Every hue, every tone, every colour...all congealed into one huge, easy-going, doing-what-was-expected, playing-by-the-rules, middle-of-the-road splatter – like a Jackson Pollack done in warm pastels. (*Beat.*) And now that I do see it...the complete portrait...I have to say in all honesty... (*Beat.*) It's not a pretty picture.

(*The lights slowly fade to BLACK.*)

Scene 2

Six months later. GRAHAM is seated at the kitchen table reading the newspaper and finishing the remainder of his breakfast. Momentarily, ELAINE appears. Standing in the doorway she stares at GRAHAM for several moments before speaking.

ELAINE: Morning, darling.

GRAHAM: (*In singsong fashion, without looking up.*) Good morning. (*Beat.*) Slept well I hope?

ELAINE: No.

> (*ELAINE meanders over to the teapot, which is sitting on the kitchen countertop, and lifts it up.*)

ELAINE: Oh…there's not much left. Shall I make a fresh pot?

GRAHAM: No, no need, darling, I'm fine – you see it off.

ELAINE: But it's no trouble.

GRAHAM: No, no, honestly, Elaine. I've had more than enough caffeine for one morning. My heart rate's high enough as it is. Wouldn't want to trigger my spasm.

ELAINE: Your what?

GRAHAM: The twitch – you remember.

> (*GRAHAM suddenly jerks his head slightly to one side in brief but violent manner.*)

ELAINE: Oh, that – yes. Well…if you're sure.

(*ELAINE proceeds to pour herself a cup of tea as GRAHAM reverts back to his newspaper. Pause.*)

GRAHAM: (*Ponderously.*) Come to think of it, I can't honestly remember the last time I *did* have a spasm. Must have got the balance right at last.

ELAINE: Balance?

GRAHAM: Of life.

(*Pause.*)

ELAINE: Graham, I… I think we need to…there's something I–

GRAHAM: Hah!

ELAINE: What?

GRAHAM: Look here.

ELAINE: What?

GRAHAM: This article.

ELAINE: Graham, I–

GRAHAM: Unbelievable!

ELAINE: (*Irritably.*) Oh, what of it?

GRAHAM: Well, according to this, some chap in Basingstoke

had been growing marijuana in his home, with lamps and what have you, and one evening he'd invited a couple of friends over for dinner, or a party of some kind. Anyway, the long and short of it is, before they left they ripped off his entire crop after he'd passed out on the sofa. So this chap goes to the police to complain, they come to his house to investigate and find just enough marijuana to charge him for possession, send him down, and now he's appealing his conviction. (*Beat.*) What a very odd world.

ELAINE: Yes, it is, but…well, I suppose sometimes…people do odd things without really thinking about what they're doing…before they do them.

GRAHAM: Nevertheless…what an idiot.

ELAINE: Well, yes…in a logical sense. (*Beat.*) But not everyone's logical all the time, Graham.

GRAHAM: Perhaps not, but why not? It makes everything so much simpler.

ELAINE: I don't know – why ask me? I suppose sometimes one's emotions get the better of one. But the fact is they're not…they're just not.

GRAHAM: Well, they should be.

ELAINE: Well, they're not; let's just leave it at that, shall we?

(*Beat.*)

GRAHAM: No, I…I truly feel quite strongly about this, actually. I mean, if one finds oneself in some sort of predicament then one has not only a duty, but a responsibility to take the most clear, logical course of action. Look at me, for instance.

ELAINE: What about you?

GRAHAM: I'm living proof. I've lived my entire life by just such a credo and it has never failed to stand me in good stead.

ELAINE: Hooray for you.

GRAHAM: For example, take that dream I had a while back. You remember – where I'd imagined myself engaged in an act of sexual…what have you, with some young male person.

ELAINE: I remember.

GRAHAM: Well, I didn't mention it at the time, but that dream became persistent…or, recurring, I should say.

ELAINE: And?

GRAHAM: And I couldn't stop thinking about it…him…us.

ELAINE: And?

GRAHAM: I became obsessed with it.

ELAINE: Oh, for God's sake, Graham…*and?*

GRAHAM: And so I did the only logical thing that one could do under the given circumstances.

(*Beat.*)

ELAINE: Which was?

GRAHAM: I sought help.

ELAINE: You what?

GRAHAM: I sought help – professional help.

ELAINE: *You?*

GRAHAM: Yes.

ELAINE: You didn't say anything.

GRAHAM: Did I not mention it?

ELAINE: No. (*Beat.*) And…what did they say?

GRAHAM: They said that…No, well, it isn't important now. The point is I did the only thing that made sense. I was in a situation beyond my control, and so took the necessary practical steps to resolve it – and in doing so I regained control.

ELAINE: What do you mean, "it's not important"? Of course it's important – tell me.

GRAHAM: Elaine, it's really not relevant to the conversation.

ELAINE: I don't care – it's relevant to me!

GRAHAM: Why?

ELAINE: Because I want to know, that's why!

(*Beat.*)

GRAHAM: Very well…after a not inconsiderable degree of psychoanalytical evaluation, I was informed that my dreams were a direct result of repressed childhood experimentation. That since I, as a boy, had never indulged in what are, apparently, all the usual same-sex activities that initial physical/sexual awakening tend to evoke, such as mutual masturbation, explorative fondling, the rubbing together of groin areas, etc., that these impulses had simply lain dormant and were only now beginning to rear themselves.

(*Beat.*)

ELAINE: I see… Actually, I don't, but…but what?

GRAHAM: What?

ELAINE: What did they advise you to do about it?

GRAHAM: The logical thing, of course.

ELAINE: Which was?

GRAHAM: To act upon my feelings in order to free myself of them.

(*Beat.*)

ELAINE: And did you?

GRAHAM: Of course I didn't.

ELAINE: No…no, of course not. (*Beat.*) And, um…and why

not?

GRAHAM: Well, darling, aside from the fact that I'm a happily married man, it's actually *not* the logical thing to do.

ELAINE: Isn't it?

GRAHAM: Absolutely not. That was then, this is now. You can't turn back the clock in an attempt to make everything as it might've been. What's done is done. You just have to move forward...go with the flow.

(*Beat.*)

ELAINE: Yes.

(*ELAINE moves to the kitchen countertop and empties the dregs of her teacup into the sink. Pause.*)

ELAINE: But...what if you can't feel it?

GRAHAM: What?

ELAINE: The flow.

GRAHAM: Well, darling, if you can't feel the flow then you can't feel life. That's what it is – that's all it is.

ELAINE: But what if it's stuck? What if yours never seems to move?

GRAHAM: But it has to move. If it didn't move how could you possibly know you were alive? It would be meaningless – there'd be no point to it.

(*Pause.*)

ELAINE: Yes. (*Beat.*) By the way, the waste disposal's stopped working again.

GRAHAM: (*With some irritation.*) Oh, not again. Whatever have you been shoving down there, darling?

ELAINE: Well…obviously something I shouldn't have.

GRAHAM: You really should be more selective about what you put in it, Elaine. One thoughtless act can affect the entire system.

ELAINE: I already know that, Graham.

GRAHAM: I don't wish to harp on, but despite the aggressive noises it makes it really is rather a delicate piece of machinery.

ELAINE: Yes. (*Beat.*) But if I spent all my time being terrified of putting things in it, to the point that I end up never putting anything in it, then one inevitably has to ask oneself why bother having it at all?

GRAHAM: I'm not suggesting that you shouldn't use it, darling, I'm merely saying that before you do use it you carefully examine whatever it is that you intend to put in it and weigh the possible consequences of such a decision.

ELAINE: Yes, well it's too late now, isn't it? The system would appear to be, indeed, compromised.

GRAHAM: Not your fault, anyway. I'm the guilty party in all of this.

ELAINE: You?

GRAHAM: Yes, for hiring that fly-by-night, cowboy outfit we had in the last time it was on the blink. I was attempting to be frugal, but as usual you get what you pay for.

(*Beat.*)

ELAINE: And pay for what you get.

GRAHAM: Anyway, no more cutting corners – this time it'll be the real thing.

(*Pause.*)

ELAINE: Perhaps we shouldn't bother.

GRAHAM: Bother with what?

ELAINE: The waste disposal.

GRAHAM: Fixing it?

ELAINE: Yes.

GRAHAM: But, darling, if we don't fix it we can't use it.

ELAINE: Would that really be such a tragedy? It's not exactly an integral part of this house – it just sits there idle most of the time.

GRAHAM: Wouldn't you miss it?

ELAINE: Would you?

GRAHAM: I'm not the one who uses it.

ELAINE: So clearly you wouldn't.

GRAHAM: Well…probably not. But it would be nice to know it's there…in case I ever did need it.

ELAINE: Well I don't think that's justification enough And quite frankly, Graham, I'm tired of it. It's always been more trouble than it's worth.

GRAHAM: But I can get a professional in – someone who knows what they're doing.

ELAINE: You tried that before, and whilst I appreciated his efforts at the time, I would have to say that the end result was an unmitigated disaster.

GRAHAM: I don't mean some ramshackle, cut-price poseur with a plunger – I'm saying let's get someone in here who really knows what they're doing.

ELAINE: And I'm saying no. I may not have a lot of experience in these things, Graham, but the gentleman you called in the last time appeared to me to be remarkably well-schooled in the tools of his trade – and at the end of the day it really didn't change the underlying problem. So I say let's forget the whole thing.

GRAHAM: But he probably did some quick-fix job on the fly.

ELAINE: That may have been his intention, but whatever the reason it still doesn't work, and, for all we know, may have made things worse. It's quite clear that the entire set-up is fundamentally flawed, so I see little point in dragging it out any further.

(*Beat.*)

GRAHAM: Well, if that's how you feel…but I do think you should mull it over before doing anything rash.

ELAINE: Oh, have no fear of that. I've mulled and pondered my way through several decades. God forbid I should do anything rash – it wouldn't be logical.

GRAHAM: Well said – that's the spirit. (*As he stands.*) Anyway, I must be off – time to earn a crust. (*After a last sip from his teacup.*) Have a splendid day, darling.

ELAINE: How could I not? A trip to the doctor's and a slog through the supermarket – I can barely contain myself.

GRAHAM: Doctor's?

ELAINE: Yes.

GRAHAM: Nothing wrong, I hope?

ELAINE: No, no just…some tests.

GRAHAM: Tests?

ELAINE: Yes. Just a…check-up.

GRAHAM: Oh…didn't know you had them.

ELAINE: Well I do. It's a woman's thing. I'm a woman, Graham.

GRAHAM: Yes – yes, of course.

ELAINE I have to go anyway – I need a refill on my sleeping pills…for all the good they do.

(*GRAHAM gives her a perfunctory kiss on the cheek.*)

GRAHAM: Well, whatever you do, do it with gusto. Remember, darling, we're only here once – have to make it count! (*As he moves to the door L.*) Must run – full day ahead!

(*GRAHAM exits. Momentarily the front door is heard closing. ELAINE stares at nothing in particular for several moments before looking over to where GRAHAM had been sitting. Pause.*)

ELAINE: Goodbye, darling – enjoy your day. (*Beat.*) Incidentally, my apologies for fucking the plumber in such close proximity to the dinner service that your sister Marjorie gave us as a wedding present. It didn't seem important at the time, but in retrospect it seems rather gauche and thoughtless. It may not be much of an excuse, but in the heat of the moment my mind was more consumed by the sensation of his penis inside of me than of long-forgotten gestures of hope and goodwill. I don't expect you to understand. I doubt Marjorie would either, given her near-religious reverence of all things bone china. (*Beat.*) I suppose you're shocked that I would even *consider* behaving in such a manner? I am too, of course. But when an opportunity like that is handed to you on a plate – even a cheap plastic one – it's very hard to say no. Especially if that's all you've ever done. (*Beat.*) Besides, before I fully realized what I was doing it was all over. I'd wanted a holiday, you see…away from everything – especially me. A long holiday in some far off place where no one knew me and I could pretend to be someone I wasn't; where I could sleep in peace for hour upon hour with nothing to disturb me. (*Beat.*)

An extended world cruise might've done the trick…breathed new life into these veins. Sadly, though, all I got was a bargain weekend break that came and went in a flash. My little holiday away from me seemed to have ended before it had even begun. (*Beat.*) I suppose all holidays are like that, aren't they? As soon as you're back home it's as if it never happened…as if you'd dreamt it. (*Pause.*) Unless, of course…you picked up a little souvenir…as a reminder.

(*The lights fade to BLACK.*)

Scene 3

Several months later. GRAHAM is seated at the kitchen table reading the newspaper and finishing the remainder of his breakfast. Presently the doorbell rings. GRAHAM, in an orderly fashion, rises from his chair and answers the front door.

GRAHAM: (*Off.*) Joy! Delighted to see you on this wonderful morning!

JOY: (*Off, impatiently.*): Yes, yes, aren't we all. Isn't it thrilling?

(*JOY enters hurriedly carrying two large shopping bags, soon followed by GRAHAM.*)

JOY: Now listen, I can't stop. I'm parked right in the middle of the bloody road thanks to your slaphappy neighbours leaving their cars at all points in between. I mean, trust me, I'm the last person in the world to give credit to the Germanic mentality, but at least they have some sense of order. Anyway, here's this week's food. (*As she begins to remove various packages from the shopping bags.*)

I'm not entirely sure what's here, but…well, various things I suppose – more or less the usual.

GRAHAM: It's really too good of you, Joy. You can't be thanked enough.

JOY: How many times must I remind you? It's not me you should be thanking, it's Svetlana. (*Beat.*) It's strange, but even though we haven't had her that long, I suddenly can't imagine life without her. She cleans the house, she does the laundry, she drags Stephen's brats around here, there and every-bloody-where as if she actually gave a damn about them, and on top of that she cooks all of this – whatever this *is* – for someone she doesn't even know. Admittedly, I've a feeling she's banging Stephen on the quiet now and then, but quite honestly, for all that she does, she's worth the price of admission.

GRAHAM: Well, I'm sure she's charming – and you must thank her for me – but nevertheless, it's you I find making delicious deliveries on my doorstep once a week, like some bountiful angel of mercy.

JOY: Christ, if I'm your idea of an angel of mercy then all I can say is God help you. Anyway, let's see what we have this week… (*As she begins transferring the packages into the freezer.*) Now, there's…Chicken Cordon Bleu…Chicken Cordon Bleu again…Beef…something – the ink's smudged…Chicken Cordon Bleu yet again – I never said she was imaginative, and finally …something completely unpronounceable, and, by the look of it, inedible. Must be one of her ethnic specialties from the Motherland. She tries to fob them off onto Stephen and I every once in a while, but of course we'll have none of it. Anyway – enjoy.

GRAHAM: How is Stephen, by the way?

JOY: Stephen? Oh, he's...there...sometimes. He's just Stephen. Why?

GRAHAM: No reason – just wondered.

JOY: God knows why – I never do. It's like wondering about the washing machine...it's just there. Anyway, if I don't move the car I'm going to–

GRAHAM: Are you happy?

(*Beat.*)

JOY: What?

GRAHAM: Are you happy...you and Stephen?

JOY: What an absurd question! How the hell should I know?

GRAHAM: Well...surely you must have some sort of idea?

(*JOY contemplates the question for a moment.*)

JOY: Nope. Sorry, Graham – haven't the foggiest. You're asking the wrong person, I'm afraid.

GRAHAM: But it's a very straightforward question – you must know?

JOY: Well I don't. I can't speak for two people. (*Beat.*) He hasn't asked for a divorce, so I suppose that's a good sign.

GRAHAM: Yes. (*Beat.*) And, um…and what about you?

JOY: What about me?

GRAHAM: Are you happy – in yourself?

JOY: Frankly, Graham, I never entertain the question – not even to myself. That way, if I am, I'm one of those fortunate souls who just don't know how lucky they are, and if I'm not, well…I'll be the last to know.

GRAHAM: But if you had to take a stab at it – like now, for instance.

JOY: Oh for heaven's sake, how does one ever know when one's happy?

GRAHAM: Well, by…by making an appraisal of one's circumstances and then…deducing some sort of approximate statement of fact.

JOY: Look, Graham, I live my life more or less in a permanent state of indifference, punctuated by the occasional thrill and the odd downer. Does that make me luckier than some half-starved human carcass in Ethiopia with flies buzzing around them? Of course it does. Should that make me happy? Probably, but the fact is I'm me and I have my own set of problems. It's all relative, isn't it?

GRAHAM: But I mean in general…in a general sense.

JOY: Well…generally speaking…I suppose…yes…all in all…I suppose I am happy…I suppose. (*Beat.*) Though even as I speak them I can't say those words ring particularly true.

GRAHAM: Good, I'm…I'm pleased.

JOY: What's gotten into you, anyway? Why are you asking these things?

GRAHAM: Oh, I don't know…just was of a mind, that's all.

JOY: Well, that's wonderful. We really must continue this at some point. Anyway, must dash!

(*JOY makes to leave.*)

GRAHAM: It's just…I thought that we were, you see – Elaine and I. More of an assumption I suppose, but…what else can you do? How does one gauge these things…until something actually happens?

JOY: Oh, Graham, must you really talk about this now? It's not that I don't want to, but if I don't–

GRAHAM: No, no, of course you must go – don't let me keep you. But…but I thought that we were, you see. And then I wake up one morning, prepared to do all the things I always do and…and I discover she's gone. (*His eyes beginning to well up.*) And I…I still don't why, really. It's not as if I did anything differently.

JOY: (*With a heavy sigh.*) Graham, must we discuss this now?

GRAHAM: (*Unaffectedly wiping the tears from the corners of his eyes.*) No, no, of course not. You run along.

(*JOY looks at her wristwatch, takes a quick look out of the window, and emits another heavy sigh before seating herself at the kitchen table.*)

JOY: First of all, I am most certainly the last person on the planet that anyone should seek any sort of counsel from, so…so whatever I just said is a sort of disclaimer. But…well, it wasn't anything you did or didn't do…necessarily…it was something she did…or all the things she didn't do…if that makes sense.

GRAHAM: I can't say that it does.

JOY: Well, she…Elaine…was afraid of life, Graham – she always was, even as a child. Not her fault, I suppose, but there it is. She was too timid to roll up her sleeves and get her hands dirty. Instead she'd always tiptoe around it, always looking in the window, too hesitant to knock on the door. And then one day she…well, I suppose she just got tired of being a spectator and decided she'd join in the fray.

GRAHAM: (*Puzzled.*) Join in the fray?

JOY: Yes.

GRAHAM: What fray?

JOY: She took a leap…into the unknown…a place she'd never been before – the place that scared her the most. I think she'd reached a point where she felt she had nothing left to lose…until she'd lost it.

GRAHAM: But I don't see how a leap…How does the taking of one's life equate to joining in the fray? What leap? It doesn't add up. I can't make sense of it…any of it.

JOY: Well, you're thinking of the second leap. I was referring to the first leap. You see, there was another leap – the original leap – before the leap that you're talking about. Which indirectly led to the second leap. This isn't making much sense, is it? I'm making her sound like a bloody frog, all this leaping about all over the place. (*Beat.*) Look, she took a leap and got a bit more than she'd bargained for. That in turn prompted the second leap, which was when she discovered that she'd...

(*JOY stops herself from continuing. Beat.*)

GRAHAM: Yes?

(*Beat.*)

JOY: No, well, it doesn't matter now.

GRAHAM: I'm sorry, Joy, I'm really very sorry, but...but it does matter. To me it does. You see, I, I...I've tried more times than I can say to piece it all together and to rationalize it all and put it into some sort of framework, some structure, but...but it won't fit. I can't find the reasoning in it. No matter what I do, none of it fits.

JOY: (*Hesitating for a moment, then decisively.*) Graham, I was not supposed to tell you this, but...well, you see...Elaine was ill. Seriously ill.

GRAHAM: (*Taken aback.*) Ill? (*Beat.*) Why...why wasn't I told?

JOY: (*Cautiously.*) I...I don't think she wanted to worry you. There was nothing you could have done.

GRAHAM: (*Bewildered.*) Nevertheless, I...What...what was it? What illness?

JOY: (*Guardedly.*) I'm...I'm not entirely sure. Some sort

of…blood disease, I believe.

GRAHAM: A blood disease? What…what sort of blood disease – what was it called?

JOY: (*With an affected sigh.*) Oh, Graham, don't ask me – I have no head for all of that tedious medical terminology. It was quite a sensation a few years back, apparently, but has since slipped from the limelight. (*Beat. To herself.*) Poor Elaine – out of step with fashion even in death.

GRAHAM: But was there no cure?

JOY: None.

GRAHAM: But…but this is the twenty-first century – surely there must have been…treatments, or…something?

JOY: (*Wearily.*) Well, yes, I suppose there were certain avenues she could have pursued that might have kept her propped up, but…well, quite honestly I think she was tired of propping herself up – she'd been doing it all her life. I think the thought of yet more propping was enough to break her back…or her will, at least.

GRAHAM: But to take one's own *life?* It's so…so damned defeatist.

JOY: In her eyes I think it had already been taken – or never been given. You must understand, it wasn't just the illness, Graham. In many respects it was simply a catalyst – an excuse, even. Something that forced her to confront something she'd been avoiding for a very long time.

GRAHAM: Which was?

JOY: Herself.

(*Beat.*)

GRAHAM: But to just…give up.

JOY: What a silly thing to say.

GRAHAM: Why? That's what she did. It's the truth.

JOY: No it isn't. She didn't give up anything. To her I think it was taking the ultimate risk…in answer to all the risks she'd never taken. Now, did it pay off? Well…only she knows that. Sometimes they do, sometimes they don't. But let's face it, are you really living anyway…if you never take risks? (*Beat.*) Still, a bit drastic, I'll grant you. Can't say I'd ever have the nerve. I could reel off an alarmingly long list of individuals whose lives I'd happily take, but my own? Don't think I'd have the balls.

(*Beat.*)

GRAHAM: She should have told me where she was – what she had. Why didn't she tell me – in plain language? Why just…do that?

JOY: A moment of madness, I suppose. We all have them now and then.

GRAHAM: Yes…quite mad.

JOY: I did try to talk her out of it, Graham – and thought I'd succeeded. Obviously the sleeping pills offered a more convincing argument than I could come up with.

(*Pause.*)

GRAHAM: I should have been told. Someone should have told me.

JOY: Yes, probably so, but…well, there's a lot of things people don't always tell each other, and there's a lot of reasons why. That's not to say that's a good thing, necessarily, I just mean that…that it's not always a bad one either. (*Beat.*) Anyway, I've told you now – against her wishes. Perhaps it'll help.

GRAHAM: Perhaps it might. (*Beat.*) Actually, I…I've a feeling there's a distinct probability that it might…at some…future juncture. (*Beat.*) Why are you so kind to me?

JOY: Me? Kind?

GRAHAM: Yes, kind. Bringing me home-cooked food every week and calling me every now and then to see if I'm all right – albeit with a tone of irritation…you still do it. Why?

(*Beat.*)

JOY: The real answer or the nice one?

GRAHAM: The real one, of course.

JOY: She asked me to.

GRAHAM: (*Attempting to mask his disappointment.*) Yes, I'd…thought as much.

(*Beat.*)

JOY: *But…* I suppose if I were being completely honest with myself – which, as you know, I've made a second career out of not doing – I'd have to say I'd have probably done it anyway. I may be as hard as nails in some ways, Graham, but I'm only human – even I thaw a little when confronted with a helpless animal. Besides which, if you ever decided, for some bizarre reason, to have your own little moment of–

(*JOY is suddenly distracted by the sound of chains and hydraulic noises coming from outside.*)

JOY: What's that noise? (*As she runs to the window.*) Oh shit! My car! (*Looking out of the window.*) They're towing my bloody car! (*At the top of her lungs as she runs through the kitchen.*) Stop, you bastards! (*As she's exiting.*) Wait! I'm here! I'm right here! (*The front door is heard being flung open. Off.*) Stop! Stop, you miserable bastards! Look, I'm here – listen to me – I'm right here! For Christ's take those bloody chains off!

(*GRAHAM, peering through the kitchen window, looks on for a moment at the unfolding drama outside.*)

GRAHAM: Oh dear. (*Beat.*) Dear, dear, dear.

(*As the disturbance subsides, GRAHAM returns to his seat at the table, pours a little more tea into his cup and resumes his perusal of the newspaper. After a while he stumbles across an article that appeals to his sense of humour. Instinctively he looks over to where ELAINE would have sat.*)

GRAHAM: Ha! Would you listen to– (*His smile soon evaporates as he realizes his error. Turning away, he stares blankly into nothingness for several moments. Then, dispassionately.)* Yes. *(Beat.)* Yes, of course. *(He reverts his attention back to the article in the newspaper. After a moment he nods his head in disbelief. Without looking up.)* Most extraordinary. *(With a sigh.)* My, my...what a very odd world.

(As he turns the page of his newspaper the lights slowly fade to BLACK.)

END OF PLAY

ABOUT THE AUTHOR

From the Royal Court Theatre in London to the Playhouse Theatre in Tasmania, the works of award-winning playwright Andrew Biss have been performed across the globe, spanning four continents. His plays have won awards on both coasts of the U.S., critical acclaim in the U.K., and quickly became a perennial sight on Off and Off-Off Broadway stages.

In London his plays have been performed at The Royal Court Theatre, Theatre503, Riverside Studios, The Pleasance Theatre, The Union Theatre, The White Bear Theatre, The Brockley Jack Studio Theatre, Fractured Lines Theatre & Film at COG ARTSpace, and Ghost Dog Productions at The Horse & Stables.

In New York his plays have been produced at Theatre Row Studios, The Samuel French Off-Off-Broadway Festival, The Kraine Theater, The Red Room Theater, Times Square Arts Center, Manhattan Theatre Source, Mind The Gap Theatre, 3Graces Theatre Company, Emerging Artists Theatre, Curan Repertory Company, Pulse Ensemble Theatre, American Globe Theatre, The American Theater of Actors, and Chashama Theatres, among others.

His plays and monologues are published in numerous anthologies from trade publishers Bedford/St. Martin's, Smith & Kraus, Inc., Pioneer Drama Service, and Applause Theatre & Cinema Books.

Andrew is a graduate of the University of the Arts London, and a member of the Dramatists Guild of America, Inc.

For more information please visit his website at:

www.andrewbiss.com

The End of the World

5M/3F Approx. 90 minutes

Valentine's parents have decided that the time has finally come for their son to leave home and discover life for himself. As he ventures forth into the vast world beyond, his new adventure is soon drawn to a halt when he is mugged at gunpoint. Frightened and exhausted, he seeks shelter at a bed and breakfast establishment named The End of the World, run by the dour Mrs. Anna. Here Valentine encounters a Bosnian woman with a hole where her stomach used to be, an American entrepreneur with a scheme to implant televisions into people's foreheads, and a Catholic priest who attempts to lure him down inside a kitchen sink. Then things start getting strange...

In this story based loosely around the state of Bardo from The Tibetan Book of the Dead - an intermediate state where the dead arrive prior to rebirth - dying is the easy part. Getting out of Bardo and returning to the land of the living is a far more perilous proposition, and unless you know what you're doing...you might never leave.

An odd, yet oddly touching tale of life, death, and the space in-between.

Leah's Gals

3M/5F Approx. 90 minutes

Leah's just won the lottery in what she describes as "the biggest single, one-time cash haul in this here dirt-poor, shitty state's history!" But, rather than living the highlife, Leah decides to split the winnings among her three daughters, asking only for a deathbed-style declaration of love in return. When her youngest daughter, Patina, scoffs at the idea, Leah disowns her with vitriolic fury. Bestowing instead the prize money upon her two eldest daughters, her dreams of a pampered retirement in the arms of her offspring for herself and her close companion, Pearl, seem guaranteed. Things soon turn sour, however, as long-held grievances and newfound wealth lead to familial treachery, violence and death.

Greed, lust, drugs, and Capodimonte combust in this low-rent, Southern fried twist on a literary classic.

The Meta Plays

A collection of short comedic plays that take theatrical conventions on a metaphysical joyride.

This unique compilation of wittily inventive short comedies can be performed by as few as 4 actors or as many as 18, all with minimal set and prop requirements. Many of these plays have gone on to receive highly successful productions around the world, garnering glowing reviews along the way.

Arcane Acts of Urban Renewal

Five One-Act Comedies Approx. 100 minutes

A collection of five thematically related, darkly humorous one-act plays in which ordinary people find themselves in the most extraordinary circumstances.

An Honest Mistake: Madge has long since surrendered herself to the verbal abuse doled out to her by her belligerent husband, Stan. On this particular evening, however, her fears of a rat beneath the floorboards, combined with her absent-mindedness, result in her dishing up Stan not only his evening meal - but also his just deserts!

A Familiar Face: Two elderly women, old friends, meet up in a London café shortly after one them – Dora – has been widowed. As Dora's grief and anger intensifies, her good friend Eydie begins to suspect there may be more to her angst than the loss of a loved one. When Dora calmly removes from her shopping bag a large glass jar containing a human head, discussions over its mysterious identity, and how it came to be lodged in the cupboard under her stairs, lead to some startling revelations.

A Slip of the Tongue: Miss Perkins, tired of the constant innuendos and sexual insinuations of her employer, Mr. Reams, has decided to hand in her notice. On this particular morning, however, Mr. Reams decides to take things one step further. Unfortunately, due to Miss Perkins' nervous disposition and a telephone that rings at a disturbingly high pitch, he soon discovers he's bitten off more than he can chew...or at least, one of them has.

An Embarrassing Odour: Ethel, a widowed pensioner, sits down one evening to tackle her daily crossword puzzle. Suddenly her tranquil world is turned upside down when a burglar enters her home, believing it to be unoccupied. As Ethel vainly attempts to forge a relationship with the violent delinquent before her, his concerns lie only with getting his hands on her valuables...that and the unpleasant smell that fills the room. What is that smell?

A Stunning Confession: During an evening in front of the television a staid married couple suddenly find themselves having to confront a new reality.

Suburban Redux

3M/1F or 2M/2F Approx. 90 minutes

After thirty years of arid matrimony and suburban monotony, Mrs. Pennington-South's only dream was that her son, Cuthbert, would break free of the cycle of upper-middle class inertia that had suffocated her. Raising him in the hope that he was homosexual, she soon begins dragging home potential suitors for tea – on this particular occasion a rather shy, awkward young man named Tristram. Cuthbert, however, finds he can no longer maintain his façade and at last confesses to his mother his guilty secret: his heterosexuality.

When Cuthbert leaves to meet Trixie, his new female friend, Mrs. Pennington-South – heartbroken but accepting – takes solace in the company of Tristram, and a mutual love of the arts soon leads to a new found friendship. After several weeks, however, Tristram's feelings take on more amorous overtones, and a confession of love for a woman almost thirty years his senior sends Mrs. Pennington-South into a state of emotional turmoil. Her anxiety is further heightened by the unexpected arrival of Cuthbert, merrily announcing that he has brought Trixie home for an introduction, and of the "big news" they wish to impart.

Mrs. Pennington-South, mortified at having to face the reality of her son's lifestyle choice, fearfully awaits the dreaded Trixie. Nothing, however, could have prepared her for what would come next.

A Ballyhoo in Blighty

The multi-award winning, critically acclaimed "Indigenous Peoples" (Winner "Best Play" – New York's Wonderland One-Act Festival) is paired with three other cheeky, uproarious comedies in what is guaranteed to be an unforgettable, side-splitting evening's entertainment.

Also included are "The Man Who Liked Dick", "Kitchen Sink Drama" and "Carbon-Based Life Form Seeks Similar" – all outrageously funny British comedies that have received lauded productions in London, New York and beyond.

Cast size: 4M / 5F (Roles can be doubled for a 2M/2F cast configuration)

Made in the USA
Columbia, SC
01 December 2020